BARCELONA
THE CITY AT A GLANCE

CU00688385

Torre Agbar
Rising from Plaça de les Glòries Cat
Jean Nouvel's multicoloured tower i
the offices of the Agbar water com,
at its most spectacular when viewed at night.
See p012

Hotel Arts
Built for the 1992 Olympic Games, the
city's first modern luxury hotel is still the
grande dame of Barcelona's seafront. Its
Pompidou-style steel exoskeleton belies
the traditional comforts that lie within.
Carrer de la Marina 19-21, T 93 221 1000

Sagrada Família
Work started in 1882 on Gaudí's unfinished
masterpiece, an enduring symbol of the
Catalan capital. The gothic basilica, which
will stand at 170m when finally complete,
is constructed from up to 30 types of stone.
Carrer de Mallorca 401, T 93 208 0414

W Hotel
Nicknamed *la vela* (the sail) for its distinctive
shape, the W is visible from all over town and
has prompted the regeneration of a previously
unkempt section of beachfront.
See p013

Santa María del Pi
Medieval architect Bartomeu Mas designed
this Barri Gòtic church's 54m-high octagonal
belfry, which was completed in the 1460s.
Plaça del Pi 7, T 93 318 4743

Castell de Montjuïc
Once a loathed fortress used as a base
to oppress the local Catalans, this castle
is now a leisure zone, hosting festivals,
outdoor film screenings and concerts.
Carretera de Montjuïc 66, T 93 256 4440

INTRODUCTION
THE CHANGING FACE OF THE URBAN SCENE

It is an exceptional thing for a city to reinvent itself so thoroughly, but Barcelona's change of fortune after the 1992 Olympics was the envy of the world. What was once considered a scruffy port town was suddenly held up as a model of urban planning, and for years there was nowhere more fashionable to spend the weekend. Then, inevitably, came the backlash, when it became the victim of its own success. Mass tourism – and rowdy antics – has overrun parts of the city and driven residents from homes, threatening to destroy the essence of what made Barcelona so alluring. In 2015, new mayor Ada Colau declared a moratorium on hotel construction and a cap on visitor numbers while the authorities devise a more sustainable model that will protect the city's culture and authenticity.

You can see why it is so popular. Its rich heritage, cutting-edge design tradition and radical cuisine are as big a draw as ever. For architecture junkies, Gaudí's modernista legacy is complemented by the work of leading global firms (Foster + Partners, EMBT and Jean Nouvel among them). And adding to a long list of excellent museums, such as the CaixaForum (see p024), CCCB (see p026) and the great art palace MNAC (Palau Nacional, Parc de Montjuïc, T 93 622 0360), Disseny Hub (see p057) opened in 2014 to showcase regional decorative and graphic arts. Spirited, style-savvy and still cool, Barcelona is much more than the Catalan capital. It simply cannot help but keep you coming back for more.

ESSENTIAL INFO

FACTS, FIGURES AND USEFUL ADDRESSES

TOURIST OFFICE
Plaça de Catalunya 17
T 93 285 3834
www.barcelonaturisme.com

TRANSPORT
Airport transfer to city centre
The Aerobús departs regularly between 5am and 1am. The journey takes 35 minutes
www.aerobusbcn.com
Car hire
Avis
T 90 211 0275
Metro
Trains run from 5am to 12am, Sunday to Thursday; 5am to 2am on Fridays; and for 24 hours on Saturdays
www.tmb.cat
Taxis
Ràdio Taxi 033
T 93 303 3033
Tourist card
A three-day Barcelona Card grants free travel and entry to many attractions

EMERGENCY SERVICES
Emergencies
T 112
Late-night pharmacy
Farmàcia Álvarez
Passeig de Gràcia 26
T 93 302 1124

CONSULATES
British Consulate-General
13th floor, Avinguda Diagonal 477
T 93 366 6200
www.gov.uk/government/world/spain
US Consulate-General
Passeig Reina Elisenda de Montcada 23
T 93 280 2227
barcelona.usconsulate.gov

POSTAL SERVICES
Post office
Correo Central
Plaça Antonio López
T 93 486 8302
Shipping
UPS (Mail Boxes Etc)
Carrer de València 214
T 93 454 6983

BOOKS
Barcelona
by Robert Hughes (Vintage)
Homage To Catalonia
by George Orwell (Penguin Classics)

WEBSITES
Architecture
www.coac.net
www.gaudi2002.bcn.es
www.rutadelmodernisme.com
Newspapers
www.elpais.com
www.lavanguardia.com

EVENTS
Barcelona Design Week
www.barcelonadesignweek.com
LOOP Fair
www.loop-barcelona.com/fair

COST OF LIVING
Taxi from El Prat Airport to city centre
€30
Cappuccino
€1.60
Packet of cigarettes
€4.85
Daily newspaper
€1.40
Bottle of champagne
€60

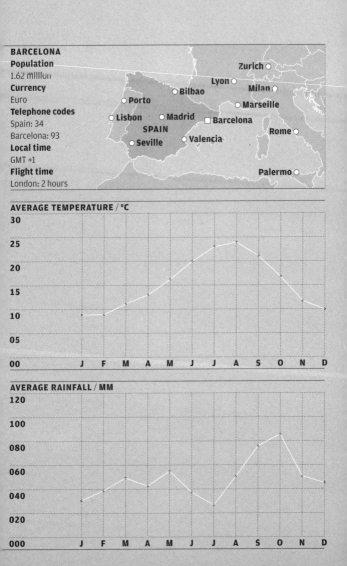

BARCELONA
Population
1.62 million
Currency
Euro
Telephone codes
Spain: 34
Barcelona: 93
Local time
GMT +1
Flight time
London: 2 hours

Zurich
Lyon
Milan
Bilbao
Marseille
Porto
Lisbon
Madrid
Barcelona
Rome
SPAIN
Seville
Valencia
Palermo

AVERAGE TEMPERATURE / °C

30
25
20
15
10
05
00

J F M A M J J A S O N D

AVERAGE RAINFALL / MM

120
100
080
060
040
020
000

J F M A M J J A S O N D

NEIGHBOURHOODS

THE AREAS YOU NEED TO KNOW AND WHY

To help you navigate the city, we've chosen the most interesting districts (see below and the map inside the back cover) and colour-coded our featured venues, according to their location; those venues that are outside these areas are not coloured.

EIXAMPLE

This sizeable district (which translates as 'extension') is where most of the city's modernista gems are located, including the Sagrada Família (see p009), Casa Milà (see p014) and Casa Batlló (see p027). The elegant Passeig de Gràcia, a power-shopping strip, cuts through the area.

BARRI GÒTIC

The most atmospheric part of Barna, the Gothic Quarter dates back to Roman times. Its winding medieval streets are lorded over by the city's main cathedral and punctuated with artisans' shops, particularly around Plaça de Sant Just and Plaça del Pi. Dine at the Michelin-starred Koy Shunka (see p052).

BARCELONETA

Replete with manmade beaches created for the Olympics, this upscale pleasure arena is awash with restaurants and bars overlooking the marina. Gentrification headed down south into Platja de Sant Sebastià with the launch of venues such as the breezy Pez Vela (see p049).

GRÀCIA

Boho and pretty, and peppered with one-off boutiques and alternative stores, Gràcia has an independent spirit and a friendly, villagey ambience, thanks to the relative lack of traffic. Nearby, check out Casa Vicens (Carrer de les Carolines 24), one of Gaudí's lesser-known buildings.

POBLE SEC

Residential and laidback, Poble Sec is a pleasant place to wander after visiting the sights and museums of Montjuïc, the city's expansive hilltop parkland. There is a string of cute cafés along Carrer de Blai, and, close by, The Box Social bistro (see p018), with a patio and garden.

POBLENOU

Upwardly mobile loft-dwelling creatives are revamping this area, carving studios out of disused warehouses and factories. To the north-east, the residential and tourist development Diagonal Mar (see p072) is the site of bold skyscrapers, but we'd favour an afternoon at Disseny Hub (see p057) and Can Framis (see p070).

RAVAL

Visit Raval to witness Barcelona's most aggressive rejuvenation over the past few years. The upper part has swapped its edgy mood for an arty one, and it is now home to the cultural centres MACBA (see p059) and Filmoteca (see p078), shops, bars and restaurants – try Dos Palillos (see p038).

SANT PERE/BORN

Museu Picasso (see p024) and the Gothic Santa María del Mar church are Born's crowd-pleasers, and the shopping here is the best in town, especially for fashion and design. Sant Pere is an up-and-coming zone; standing proud as its centrepiece is the Mercat de Santa Caterina (see p072).

LANDMARKS
THE SHAPE OF THE CITY SKYLINE

It took half a decade before Barcelona rose from the depths of the recession that put so many projects on hold. The recovery has seen a number of major developments, notably the restoration of the Hospital de la Santa Creu i Sant Pau (Carrer de Sant Antoni Maria Claret 167, T 93 291 9000), an art nouveau complex encompassing 27 pavilions, gardens and tunnels built from 1902 to 1930, created by Lluís Domènech i Montaner. El Born Centre Cultural (Plaça Comercial 12, T 93 256 6851) is a rejuvenation of the 1876 market, Barcelona's first iron building under whose sweeping canopy is an archaeological site that dates from 1700. And then there are the 21st-century landmarks of Torre Agbar (see p012), Disseny Hub (see p057) and Mercat dels Encants (see p073) that anchor the transformation of Les Glòries from chaotic junction to park. From here, the Avinguda Diagonal artery that slices up the city carries on to the coast and 2004's Universal Forum of Cultures, the site of Herzog & de Meuron's triangular Edifici Fòrum (Parc del Fòrum).

Amid all this upheaval it is comforting to cling to the familiar. Make your way to the fantastical roof of Gaudí's Casa Milà (see p014) and, if you would rather dodge the hawkers at the Sagrada Família (Carrer de Mallorca 401, T 93 208 0414), instead discover his Torre Bellesguard (Carrer de Bellesguard 16, T 93 250 4093), a gothic-modernist masterpiece that was only unveiled in 2013. *For full addresses, see Resources.*

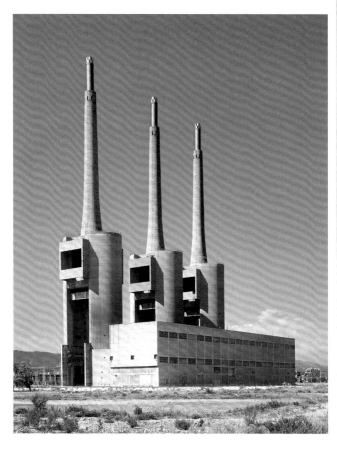

Tres Chimeneas

Looming behind Port Fòrum on the north seafront is an endangered relic of the city's industrial past. The thermoelectric power plant built for Fecsa-Endesa in the 1970s is unmissable due to its three 200m concrete towers with 20m steel caps that make it the tallest structure on the Med. Despite polluting this stretch of beach for decades – it has chillingly been dubbed Playa Chernobyl – the Three Chimneys have claimed a place in local folklore, and residents saved the facility from demolition when it ceased operation in 2011. Municipal authorities are now deciding what to do with it. The hope is that, rather than real-estate development, it could be converted into a large cultural complex that preserves something of its historical significance.
Port Forum, Sant Adrià de Besòs

Torre de Comunicaciones de Montjuïc

Even those who deride Santiago Calatrava cannot deny the allure of his futuristic steel beacon. Standing proud at 136m and adorned with Gaudí-style *trencadís* at its base, it serves as a giant sundial that casts the time on Plaça d'Europa. The fluid form is representative of an athlete holding the Olympic flame, but locals christened it *el pirulí* (the lollipop). It was completed in 1992 just in time to transmit TV coverage of the Games. Telefónica still undertakes operations from here, but the enormous ground-floor installations – a circular auditorium and open-air terraces – had been in disuse almost since the Olympics concluded. In 2012, the mobile giant began tapping the site's potential, and the rehabilitated spaces now host film shoots, private events and conventions. *Passeig de Minici Natal 8*

Torre Agbar

French architect Jean Nouvel's 142m-tall structure became a defining feature of the Barcelona skyline after its completion in 2005. Unless you are a prospective tenant of the offices inside, it's unlikely you'll gain access to the steel-and-glass interior. Instead, it is best to appreciate the 4,500-windowed tower from Plaça de les Glòries Catalanes (see p073). Agbar is Barcelona's water company, which Nouvel seldom tired of referencing in the design The sensuous exterior resembles a bubbling stream – its surface appears to ripple under a liquid film. The top floors are clad in clear glass, below which metal strips descend in tones of white and blue, before meeting the burnt orange, fuchsia and fiery red panels that rise from the base. *Plaça de les Glòries Catalanes, www.torreagbar.com*

W Hotel

Barcelona architect Ricardo Bofill (see p063) is one of Spain's most prolific and inventive. Yet despite his global status, his hometown projects are surprisingly few. Two major works in 2009 addressed that: the elegant airport terminal and the W. The soaring, sail-shaped hotel sits at the point where the city's beach ends, and, together with Hotel Arts (see p016), it bookends this stretch of sand. The W is the more arresting of the two: at 90m high and with a silver glass facade, it is the first distinguishable form that many visitors see, whether they arrive by air or by sea. The project, which also includes a boardwalk and a generous plaza, all by Bofill, has opened up a little pocket of the city's precious shoreline.
Plaça de la Rosa dels Vents 1,
T 93 295 2800, www.w-barcelona.com

Casa Milà

This iconic 1912 residential building, with its wave-like facade, was Gaudí's last civil project before he secluded himself at the site of the Sagrada Família (see p009). Take a tour of the most important areas: a flat fitted out in the modernista decor of the era, the roof, an exhibition space, and the Espai Gaudí – a showcase of the architect's creations – in the attic.

Carrer Provença 261-265, T 90 220 2138

HOTELS

WHERE TO STAY AND WHICH ROOMS TO BOOK

The city brims with great hotels and the competition keeps the best on their toes. A fresh breed of laidback glamour that is embodied by DO (see p023) and The Serras (Passeig de Colom 9, T 93 169 1868) has overshadowed earlier design-led ventures such as Hotel Claris (Carrer de Pau Claris 150, T 93 487 6262) and Hotel Arts (Carrer de la Marina 19-21, T 93 221 1000). To keep their clientele, these establishments have invested in top restaurants: Arts' two-Michelin-starred Enoteca (T 93 483 8108), hip Roca Moo at Hotel Omm (Carrer del Rosselló 265, T 93 445 4000), whose 1950s-style lounge is as popular as ever, and Moments (T 93 151 8781) at the sophisticated Mandarin Oriental (Passeig de Gràcia 38-40, T 93 151 8888), set in a 1950s bank with Patricia Urquiola interiors.

Axel (Carrer d'Aribau 33, T 93 323 9393) is still Eixample's most gay-friendly luxury hotel, which is saying something, and equally as eclectic are Vincci Bit (Carrer de Josep Pla 69, T 93 165 7420) and Vincci Gala (Ronda de Sant Pere 32, T 93 508 3200). Period splendour can be found at Bagués (see p022) and Cotton House (see p020). Meanwhile, original enterprises such as Hotel Brummell (see p018), Praktik Hotel Bakery (Carrer de Provença 279, T 93 488 0061) and yök Casa + Cultura (Carrer de Trafalgar 39, T 64 062 5313), three eco-friendly apartments in a renovated 1900 building, are shaking up the boutique scene.

For full addresses and room rates, see Resources.

El Palauet

Truly noble accommodation can be found in this modernista mansion transformed into six sumptuous self-catering suites. Dating from 1906, it was designed by Pere Falqués, whose most famous work is the iron streetlighting on Passeig de Gràcia. El Palauet exposes all the excesses of the epoch, with elaborately carved woodwork, moulded ceilings and delicate leadlight throughout. The proprietors have updated the edifice admirably, installing high-tech lighting, bespoke Corian bathrooms and a creamy decor that features pieces from Starck, Jacobsen and Eames, among other important 20th-century designers. The best rooms, such as the Principal Tibidabo Suite (above), which has a pretty, stained-glass *glorieta* (sun room), face the rear. *Passeig de Gràcia 113, T 93 218 0050, www.elpalauet.com*

Hotel Brummell

This true urban oasis is tucked away behind an unassuming facade in Poble Sec. The 1870s building was remodelled by architect Inma Rábano and decorated by Australian duo Blankslate, who took inspiration from Geoffrey Bawa's lyrical tropical modernism, adding antiques from Europe and local artworks to a backdrop of cool greys and ice blues. The ground floor spills onto a courtyard that centres around a concrete water bowl from Sri Lanka, overlooked by a pool deck from where you can watch life unfold in the surrounding apartments. The Montjuïc-facing penthouses have open-air bathtubs on their private terraces. Though amenities are limited, they do include chef Damien Bolger's fresh cuisine at The Box Social (T 63 533 4453) and bike rental.
Nou de la Rambla 174, T 93 125 8622, www.hotelbrummell.com

Mercer Hotel

A world removed from the tourist bustle a short walk away, the Mercer, a sympathetic reimagining of a building that has parts dating back to the Roman era, gives off a cool, high-ceilinged calm. Fittingly for a hotel located in the middle of Barri Gòtic, the design – overseen by architect Rafael Moneo – incorporates an excess of original features. These include wooden coffered ceilings, bare stone walls, gothic windows, medieval columns and a Roman-period watchtower, which was once part of the walls that circled the city. Neutral-toned rooms, such as the Junior Suite (above), overlook a central orange-tree-flanked patio, addressing the lack of natural light common to buildings in this quarter. For direct sun, head up to the rooftop pool. *Carrer dels Lledó 7, T 93 310 2387, www.mercerbarcelona.com*

Cotton House Hotel

The splendour in which the city's merchant class used to live is evident in the old HQ of the cotton guild. Within the emblematic 1879 building, designed by Elies Rogent, Lázaro Rosa-Violán has married original neoclassical features – geometric tiles, boiserie panelling and fine ceiling frescoes (above) – with contemporary furnishings and artworks. The crowning glory is a 1957 spiral staircase (opposite) suspended from the roof by metal rods. Rooms have huge beds and fine cotton, of course; those on upper floors offer monochrome interiors and look out over the calmer courtyard side. You'll find Catalan cuisine at Batuar (T 93 450 5046), a regal afternoon tea in the library lounge, and a rooftop pool with views of Sagrada Família, best at sunset. *Gran Via de les Corts Catalanes 670, T 93 450 5045, www.hotelcottonhouse.com*

Bagués Hotel

Situated within an 1850 mansion that was designed by the Catalan architect Josep Fontserè i Domènech, this bijou property pays homage to its former occupants, the Bagués-Masriera jewellers, at almost every turn. There's a mosaicked reception desk, gilded hallways, and even a tiny museum displaying enamel work from the family's centuries-old collection. Of the 31 rooms, the Jewel Suite (above) is the diamond in the crown. Madagascan ebony and gold leaf accents marry with original Masriera modernist gems, and there is also a small balcony, solarium and spa. The rooftop terrace has a pool and a hip bar where youthful Barcelonians meet for after-work tipples. We suggest a Gin Mare, distilled locally in Vilanova, with tonic.
La Rambla 105, T 93 343 5000,
www.derbyhotels.com

Hotel DO: Plaça Reial

'Boutique hotel' is an exhausted phrase these days, but the DO exemplifies the concept; a small, stylish, family-owned establishment comprising just 18 rooms (Junior Suite, above). A 2011 renovation was overseen by architect Oriol Bohigas; the interior design is by Lázaro Rosa-Violán and the result is a sophisticated affair, utilising mismatched pieces of furniture, hardwood floors, reclaimed beams and colourful rugs – even the stationery trays are covetable. Unusually, breakfast, the (non-alcoholic) contents of the minibar, wi-fi and an hour in the sauna and steam room are included in the rate. Situated just off La Rambla, it has a roof terrace with a plunge pool and fine views of the arcaded Plaça Reial and the city beyond. *Plaça Reial 1, T 93 481 3666,*
www.hoteldoreial.com

24 HOURS

SEE THE BEST OF THE CITY IN JUST ONE DAY

Barcelona has such a captivating range of attractions that, on first foray, you can only scratch the surface. It would be impertinent not to pay respect to Gaudí's genius, and you can tick off Casa Battló (see p027) and more along Passeig de Gràcia. MACBA (see p059) is a must for modern art, and Disseny Hub (see p057) consolidates the design and decorative arts museums. If you are interested in heritage, head to the Palau de la Música (Carrer Palau de la Música 4-6, T 93 295 7200) and Museu Picasso (Carrer de Montcada 15-23, T 93 256 3000). Up the Montjuïc hillside is Fundació Joan Miró (see p066) and the reassembly of Mies van der Rohe's modernist vision (see p028). Nearby, the CaixaForum (Avinguda de Francesc Ferrer i Guàrdia 6-8, T 93 476 8600) puts on touring exhibitions.

Recharge with a frosty one at Fàbrica Moritz (Ronda de Sant Antoni 39-41, T 93 426 0050), the beer brand's epic resurrection of its 1856 factory. Jean Nouvel has created a labyrinth of glowing amber, resin-preserved mosaics, vaulted concrete and restored brickwork. Or head to Albert Adrià's enclave for a *vermut* at Bodega 1900 (Carrer de Tamarit 91), before dinner at any one of his four restaurants (see p042). Then find a cocktail den in Barri Gòtic, Born or Raval, as it is not worth going dancing until 2am, when storied Sala Apolo (Carrer Nou de la Rambla 113, T 93 441 4001) and Sala Razzmatazz (Carrer de Pamplona 88, T 93 320 8200) come to life. *For full addresses, see Resources.*

10.00 Satan's Coffee Corner

Marcos Bartolomé effectively kickstarted the artisan coffee movement in the city. Having debuted as a takeaway counter in a Raval gift shop in 2012, Satan's Coffee Corner now occupies a light-filled space nestled in Barri Gòtic. Bartolomé has traded a traditional service counter for an open floorplan and communal island bench, dressed with limited-edition art prints, succulents and packaged beans from roaster Right Side, all available to buy. A creative menu rotates to match the blend of the week. In the morning, have a brew accompanied by a bagel, muesli or chia pudding, or opt for takeout – cups are adorned with illustrations in the style of the owner's tattoos. Alternatively, pop by later for oysters and craft beer.
Arc de Sant Ramon del Call 11,
T 666 222 599, www.satanscoffee.com

11.30 CCCB

Spanish architects Albert Viaplana and Helio Piñón renovated the Casa de Caritat almshouse in 1994, adding a glass facade to create what has now become a cultural hub for art and music. As well as curating a busy programme of some of the most absorbing exhibitions in town, Centre de Cultura Contemporània de Barcelona, to give it its full name, hosts a cross-section of multidisciplinary festivals, debates, lectures, concerts and courses. During August it presents Gandules, a series of outdoor cinema screenings, showing often overlooked films from around the world. Combine with a visit to next-door contemporary art museum MACBA (see p059), designed by Richard Meier, which displays Catalan and international work. *Carrer de Montalegre 5, T 93 306 4100, www.cccb.org*

13.00 Casa Batlló

The Illa de la Discòrdia (Block of Discord) is home to four key modernista buildings in wildly different styles (hence the name). Casa Mulleras (No 37), designed by Enric Sagnier, Casa Amatller (No 41), by Josep Puig i Cadafalch, and Casa Lleó Morera (see p089) complete the quartet, but the centrepiece is Casa Batlló, one of Gaudí's most distinctive builds – a renovation of an existing structure finished in 1906. The *trencadís* (broken tile) mosaic that blankets the facade is mesmerising, as is the surreal, undulating interior. Among the highlights are the spine-like stairwell; the drawing room and its stained-glass windows that have sinuous frames; and the shimmering, tile-clad roof, said to represent the dragon slain by Catalonia's patron saint, Jordi. *Passeig de Gràcia 43, T 93 216 0306, www.casabatllo.es*

15.30 Pavelló Mies van der Rohe

This iconic monument to rationalism, built as the German Pavilion for the 1929 Barcelona World's Fair, is seen as a milestone in modern European architecture. All marble, onyx, steel and glass, it is the proper home for Mies van der Rohe's 'Barcelona' chair. The pavilion was disassembled in 1930, but in 1980, Oriol Bohigas, then head of urban planning at the city council, began to appoint a team to research, design and oversee its reconstruction. Ignasi de Solà-Morales, Cristian Cirici and Fernando Ramos were the selected architects. Work began in 1983 and the new building was opened on its original site in 1986. Open 10am to 8pm daily; guided tours take place on Saturdays. *Avinguda Francesc Ferrer i Guàrdia 7, T 93 423 4016, www.miesbcn.com*

17.00 43 The Spa

Located on the 43rd floor of Hotel Arts (see p016), this sun-soaked retreat is not to be missed for its stunning views of the Mediterranean. The spa uses the Spanish skincare brand Natura Bissé, and offers two signature treatments, including the 43 Experience, €200, a unique massage that incorporates numerous chiropractic techniques, pressure, stretching and precious aromatherapy oils. Others are faithful to the seafront environment – a marine algae eye treatment is superb for diminishing post-flight puffiness and dark circles. Facilities include hydrotherapy pools, steam rooms and baths, saunas and a relaxation area with outdoor terraces (above). Do book well ahead, though, as the hotel guests have priority here. *Carrer de la Marina 19-21, T 93 221 1000, www.hotelartsbarcelona.com*

21.30 El Velódromo

This Barcelona institution reopened in 2009 as El Velódromo, having been a much-loved meeting point and *casino* (as in social club, not gambling den) from 1933 to 2000. Inside one of Barcelona's few true art deco buildings, it's a gem of a bar/restaurant, meticulously restored to recall the grandeur of the early 20th century. Pistachio-painted columns, lime-green banquettes, marble-tiled floors and an ornately carved and polished wood ceiling create an attractive backdrop to the menu, which is overseen by Michelin-starred chef Jordi Vilà. Far removed from the well-trodden trails of downtown, and open from 6am to 3am, it is no surprise that locals have reclaimed this haunt as their own, and it is always buzzing, from early in the morning until late at night. *Carrer de Muntaner 213, T 93 430 6022*

URBAN LIFE

CAFÉS, RESTAURANTS, BARS AND NIGHTCLUBS

The birth of Barcelona's distinct style of Catalan cuisine is thanks largely to the success of the culinary mecca elBulli, which closed in 2011. While its chef Ferran Adrià shifted his focus to a gastronomic research centre, brother Albert Adrià, who cooked at the restaurant for 23 years, has forged an empire in Sant Antoni, revolutionising the scene with casual venues and more accessible prices, from the revamped Tickets (see p051) to the sublime Pakta (see p042).

The nearby Carrer del Parlament area is brimming with creative kitchens such as Tarannà (Carrer de Viladomat 23, T 93 106 1193), and tapas is a must at Bar Cañete (Carrer de la Unió 17, T 93 270 3458), while the paella and smoky rice dishes of the beachfront Kaiku (Plaza del Mar 1, T 93 221 9082) are hard to beat. And you'll be spoilt for choice at El Nacional (Passeig de Gràcia 24, T 93 518 5053), which houses four restaurants and four bars in a splendid 1889 building, restored in art deco style by Lázaro Rosa-Violán.

The blue-and-white-tiled Xixbar (Carrer de Rocafort 19, T 93 423 4314), a former creamery, is spurring the fervour for *gintónics*, and the new wave of cocktail bars is led by Bobby Gin (Carrer de Francisco Giner 47, T 93 368 1892) and the artsy Collage (Carrer dels Consellers 4, T 93 179 3785). The classy speakeasy Dry Martini (Carrer d'Aribau 162-166, T 93 217 5072), incongruously located in a 1970s block of flats, has long been a haunt of the intelligentsia. *For full addresses, see Resources.*

Barton

In the upper stretches of Eixample, Barton is known for its sophisticated raw food, but also serves classic Catalan dishes and innovative tapas. Signature dishes include the raw wheat pizza with cashews, cheese and oregano, and the San Sebastián-style hake with potato foam. Architect Magüi Gonzalez and designer Isabel Lopez Vilalta have created an ambience that reflects the culinary range, melding the contemporary, in the form of Arik Levy's delicate graphic 'Wireflow' pendant lighting system, to the traditional – felt-upholstered walls that provide insulation and an open pantry of reclaimed wood that gives a nod to taverns of yore. Through the glass facade, watch locals going about their business in one of the city's more authentic neighbourhoods. *Carrer de Londres 103, T 93 414 5929, www.bartonbcn.com*

Mitja Vida

The three friends responsible for the Morro Fi blog opened their own tapas bar in 2010, spearheading the revival of vermouth – a fortified, aromatic wine of Italian origin that caught on as an aperitif a century ago. In Barcelona, it was traditionally imbibed before Sunday lunch to whet the appetite, but Morro Fi and now Mitja Vida, a concrete cube that is a contemporary incarnation of a classic tavern, have encouraged its popularity among hip thirty-somethings throughout the week. The anchovy-stuffed olives in paprika vinaigrette are legendary here, as are the salty pickled morsels and seafood *conservas*, without which the art of the *vermuteo* would be incomplete. Host your own sessions with the takeaway kits, which include house-brand olives, green chillis and bottles designed by Martí Guixé. *Carrer de Brusi 39, www.morrofi.cat*

Bar Nou

The quintessentially Catalan snack of *pa amb tomàquet* finds its most modern iteration in Bar Nou, where the spreading of tomato on bread is taken as seriously as the graphic identity and interior design. Miguel Àngel Vaquer has distilled the essence of this local dish and opened it up to a range of possibilities. Combine plump hanging tomatoes with your choice of bread, olive oil and salt, try contemporary twists like tomato-rubbed tortilla pretzel or *bagel de butifarra*, or tuck into new versions of classic, hearty meals, such as *macarrones gratinados* and garlic soup. The crisp space by MAIO studio, featuring neon signs and a wood rendition of a typical ceiling vault, as well as soundtracks by Discos Paradiso, attract hipster locals. Open until midnight, it's a refuge from the touristy chains that dominate the area.
Ronda Universitat 13, T 93 667 0506, www.barnou.cat

Dos Palillos

The Michelin-starred Dos Palillos perfectly encapsulates two citywide trends: Asian cuisine and creative interpretations of tapas (*palillo* means both toothpick and chopstick). Chef Albert Raurich and his Japanese wife, Tamae Imachi, both former members of the elBulli team, have created a happy marriage of East and West in their tiny restaurant. The front bar pays homage to traditional tapas haunts, thanks to the strip lighting, terrazzo flooring and kitsch paraphernalia. Beyond it is a dark dining room (above) that is space-challenged, but does work as an intimate setting for the intricate food, which includes dishes such as tuna *temaki*, and Chinese-style prawn and Ibérico pork belly dumplings, which are made with potato flour.

Carrer d'Elisabets 9, T 93 304 0513, www.dospalillos.com

Boca Grande

Another project from interior designer Lázaro Rosa-Violán – who is also behind Hotel Praktik Bakery (see p016), Cotton House Hotel (see p020) and Hotel DO (see p023) – Boca Grande bears the hallmarks of his opulent yet cosy eclecticism. The seating in the wood-panelled restaurant is plushly upholstered, and surfaces are strewn with antiques, old photographs and sketches. The most spectacular space is the downstairs bathroom, with vintage mirrors and banquettes, and it thumps to a DJ mix. The seafood-leaning menu includes dishes such as scallops with Iberian ham. There's also a cocktail room and oyster bar, and upstairs is Boca Chica (above), a lavish bar with a colonial air. On the floor above that, lounge-style The Apartment has a terrace. *Passatge de la Concepció 12, T 93 467 5149, www.bocagrande.cat*

Saboc

Its former incarnation Bestiari was known for its creative Mediterranean cuisine, and Saboc carries on that legacy in an updated interior. Architects Juan Carlos Fernández, Adam Bresnick and Reyes Castellano have given it a Scandinavian feel with nods to its locality, melding materials such as plywood with floor tiles that mimic those of Passeig de Gràcia, as well as mustard-coloured armchairs by Hay and pendant lamps by Lightyears. The menu covers four cooking techniques: raw, low temperature, stove and griddle. Order one of each – sea bass ceviche; egg cooked at 62°C; risotto with asparagus and prawn casserole; and beef *tataki* with tomato petals. In what can be an overpriced part of town, €25 here will buy some very fine dining.
Carrer de la Fusina 3, T 93 268 3080, www.saboc.com

Poncelet Cheese Bar

Following the success of its first venture in Madrid, artisan cheese-maker Poncelet opened this outpost in 2014. Occupying a large area on the ground floor of the Meliá Sarrià Hotel, the restaurant/bar/lounge is an exercise in colour and form by Valencia firm EstudiHac, whose heterogeneous, geometric design was actually inspired by the mathematician Jean-Victor Poncelet. There's even a diamond-shaped pantry,

while all tables have views of the vertical garden. Try the Manchego cheese bonbons, gnocchi and fondue, or visit the sinuous bar to witness the experts slice one of 140 types of cheese, which hail from Spain and across Europe. They are each served with bread, chutneys and jams, and come with suggested pairings of wine, beer or cava. *Avinguda de Sarrià 50, T 93 249 2200, www.ponceletcheesebar.es*

Pakta

Part of Albert Adrià's dining dynasty, Pakta specialises in Nikkei cuisine, a fusion of Japanese and Peruvian style. Two tasting menus offer vibrant, exotic dishes typified by gold-leaf meringue with Pisco-flavoured *dulce de leche* ice cream. El Equipo Creativo designed the venue as a Japanese tavern, wrapped in yarn panels inspired by Peruvian looms.
Carrer de Lleida 5, www.pakta.es

Disfrutar

This is elBulli for the people. Opened by three of its former head chefs, Disfrutar, meaning 'to enjoy', serves up the thrill of haute cuisine at decent prices. After a welcome cocktail, which most likely will involve foam, choose between the two tasting menus – 17 courses for €68 or 25 courses for €98 – that include delicacies such as liquid olives, transparent ravioli, beetroot meringue, or chocolate chillies.

Interiors are delightfully down-to-earth in contrast, thanks to El Equipo Creativo's placement of colourful ceramic tiles and perforated earth bricks in bold geometric patterns. A streetside gastrobar with black metal framing leads past an open-plan kitchen to an airy courtyard-facing dining area with landscaped nooks and skylights.
Carrer de Villarroel 163, T 93 348 6896, ca.disfrutarbarcelona.com

Lando

Located on a quiet alley off uber-cool Carrer del Parlament, Lando opened in 2014. The triple arched entrance of the former garage leads into an airy dining room designed by local studio Decorner. Concrete floors, white-tiled walls and bespoke wooden tables marry industrial New York minimalism with European charm. Set day and night menus – with vegan options – change fortnightly and offer predominantly French-influenced Mediterranean dishes, conceived with the advice of chef Bernard Benbassat, who specialises in macrobiotic cuisine. Snack on marrow with spiced cookie crunch or moules marinières at the bar, or settle in for suckling lamb rib with faux-cabbage kimchi, followed by *torrija* (French toast) served with light citrus crème and almond ice cream.

Passatge Pere Calders 6, T 93 348 5530, www.lando.es

Chivuo's

In Barcelona and indeed much of Spain, the humble sandwich, or *bocata*, rarely amounts to more than a lone cut of meat slapped inside a semi-stale baguette. Not so at Chivuo's. Venezuelans Alejandro Bringas and Juan Andrés Lattuf met while cooking at Negro-Rojo (T 93 405 9444), and serve up 'slow street food' prepared in their small kitchen. The limited but mouthwatering menu is inspired by good old-fashioned US grub, featuring comfort dishes such as classic Philly Cheese steak, burgers with onion marmalade, bacon and provolone, tuna melts and a pulled pork and aioli sandwich. Wash it down with a craft beer from a local brewery. It's a hip, lively venue, decked out in wood and featuring graphic art by Xavier Sánchez.
Carrer del Torrent de l'Olla 175,
T 93 218 5134, www.chivuos.com

Pez Vela

Another success from Grupo Tragaluz's stable of restaurants and hotels, Pez Vela dropped anchor in 2011 down at the southern tip of Platja de Sant Sebastià. It has two parts: an industrial-chic interior of exposed pipes, white steel panels and lacquered corrugated iron, where a slick bar specialises in bespoke cocktails; and a breezy, relaxed seaside terrace (above), where one might retreat for lunch after spending a morning on the beach. At any time, the simple menu offers a decent range of paellas, tapas and chargrilled meat or fish. Book in advance to secure an outdoor table. In the evenings, you'll be rubbing shoulders with a mix of savvy locals and party people staying at the nearby W Hotel (see p013).
Passeig Mare Nostrum 19-21,
T 93 221 6317, www.grupotragaluz.com

Jaime Beriestain Café

Barcelona-based Chilean designer Jaime Beriestain conceived his concept store and café as an extension of his home. The place is like a real-life Pinterest board of his favourite objects – midcentury design, Dibbern glassware and Heeley fragrances are sold alongside his own pieces, which cover an astonishing spectrum, from retro armchairs to contemporary rugs, reissues of vintage lighting, tableware, sunglasses, stationery and gourmet products. In the café, which is decked out with intricate parquetry, velvet seating and 1960s Italian chandeliers, chef Pedro Salillas updates the local cuisine with cosmopolitan notes, in dishes such as granny's onion soup, and seafood marinated in sesame, wasabi and lime, and vegan and low-cal options.
Carrer de Pau Claris 167, T 93 515 0782, www.beriestain.com

Tickets

In 2011, super-chef Ferran Adrià and his brother Albert breathed culinary life into an ordinary part of town with the opening of Tickets and adjoining 41° Experience. The latter has since closed, while it moves to a new location in Albert Adrià's Enigma, which launches in 2016, and enabling the expansion of the highly popular Tickets. It still offers tapas in a playful space, serving traditional morsels as well as the signature molecular cuisine – manchego foam with a mini airbag – and now incorporates La Dolça, a fanciful dessert area with doily tabletops, pastel chairs and a strawberry-strewn ceiling. Also in the area and run by Albert Adrià are Pakta (see p042) and the casual *taquería* Niño Viejo (T 93 348 2194). For all of these, book well ahead, online. *Avinguda del Paral·lel 164, www.ticketsbar.es*

Koy Shunka

Hideki Matsuhisa's haute Mediterranean/ Asian fusion space has proved to be one of the city's most successful restaurant launches of the past few years. Interior designer Pedro Cortacans made a focal point of the Japanese *kappo*-style open kitchen, and a spot at the large, U-shaped bar provides the ultimate perch if you're dining alone or *à deux*. A further 30 or so seats are spread across the dining room.

Koy Shunka's clever dishes are Japanese, Spanish or a skilful mix of the two, such as the Wagyu beef with Catalan *múrgulas* (morels) or tempura scallops. No wonder many of the finest chefs in the country, including Ferran Adrià – a fan since the early days – can be found kicking back at the bar while Matsuhisa orders for them. *Carrer de Copons 7, T 93 412 7939, www.koyshunka.com*

INSIDER'S GUIDE

MIREIA RUIZ, GRAPHIC DESIGNER

Cofounder of the design studio Cocolia (www.cocolia.cat), Mireia Ruiz grew up in the seaside town of Castelldefels and moved to Barcelona in 2010. 'I just feel good here,' she says. 'And it's warm too.' She lives in the residential *barri* of Les Corts. 'I love how every district has a distinct style. My favourite is Gràcia. It has a village vibe despite being in the heart of the city.'

For local fashion, Ruiz suggests La Tercera (Carrer del Brosolí 4, T 62 530 1796), for the slouchy tapered trousers and tasseled bags, and shoes from De Ubieta (Carrer de Sant Pere Mitjà 70, T 93 106 0784). She browses for design objects at Studiostore (Carrer del Comerç 17, T 93 222 5075). You might find her at neighbourhood pizzeria La Capricciosa (Carrer de Viladomat 261 and 265, T 93 410 2040) or Strata Bakery (Carrer de Provença 158, T 93 451 1309). Ruiz is also a regular at the family-run Envalira (Plaça del Sol 13, T 93 218 5813), where she recommends the *arroz a la milanesa*.

Saturday is spent looking for treasures at Mercat dels Encants (see p073) before evening cocktails at Surf House (Carrer l'Almirall Aixada 22, T 93 250 7023), perhaps after hiring out a paddleboard. She will spend Sunday decompressing at Parc de l'Oreneta (Carrer de Montevideo 45), a forest on the north-west fringes of the city where Bellavista (Mirador Forestal, T 60 074 8470) serves a mighty roast chicken and has a gorgeous terrace overlooking Barcelona. *For full addresses, see Resources.*

ART AND DESIGN

GALLERIES, STUDIOS AND PUBLIC SPACES

The creative cauldron of modernisme at the beginning of the 20th century and the avant-garde movements that followed established Barcelona as one of Europe's most dynamic art hubs, producing legendary figures such as Antoni Gaudí, Joan Miró, Salvador Dalí and Pablo Picasso. Much of their oeuvre adorns the city – you'll find Picasso's engravings on the Col·legi d'Arquitectes (see p080) and Miró's *Dona i Ocell* in his eponymous park (Carrer d'Aragó 2). After WWII, Antoni Tàpies (see p068) was considered to be the new pioneer. Although the scene today struggles to recover from the economic crisis, and lacks public funding, a handful of institutions, including Arts Santa Mònica (see p058), promote emerging talent, as do many private galleries, from Trama (Carrer de Petritxol 5, T 93 317 4877) to Artevistas (Passatge del Crèdit 4, T 93 513 0465).

Local design, by contrast, has been basking in the limelight ever since the Olympics, when the furniture of Javier Mariscal and Oscar Tusquets, cofounder of the BD collective (Carrer de Ramon Turró 126, T 93 457 0052), came to the attention of the world and pushed Barcelona to the forefront of the industry. Big names such as Antoni Arola, Martí Guixé and Curro Claret followed suit, and in more recent years, a return to artisan techniques has found its expression in the gracefully imperfect ceramics of Xavier Mañosa (see p081) and the wooden stools of Marc Morro (see p084). *For full addresses and opening times, see Resources.*

Disseny Hub

Anticipated since 2001, the Disseny Hub opened in 2014 to consolidate all of the city's collections of Spanish costume and textiles, graphic and decorative arts, and ceramics. The commanding zinc- and glass-clad building, which has been nicknamed *la grapadora* (the stapler) for the way that it dramatically cantilevers over Plaça de les Glòries Catalanes, is the creation of local architects MBM. Two of its floors are 14.5m below ground, yet are still illuminated by natural light via a clever trench system that incorporates a lake. A polychromatic LED lighting system makes for dynamic exhibition spaces (Sala A, above), which display more than 70,000 objects dating from the 4th century, for example, Barba Corsini's curvilinear 1955 'Pedrera' chair. *Plaça de les Glòries Catalanes 37-38, T 93 309 1540, www.dhub-bcn.cat*

Arts Santa Mònica

This unconventional institution is one of the more authentic venues on La Rambla. One of the few remaining intact convents, the 1636 monument was inaugurated in 1988 as a space for cross-disciplinary and multimedia installations. It puts on more than 20 exhibitions a year – including US photographer Jessica Lange's 'Unseen' (above) – that span the realms of music, cinema, fashion, photography, theatre, dance, architecture and science. It was remodelled in 1990 by Helio Piñón and Albert Viaplana, who preserved much of the original structure, including the arched atrium. A renovation in 2009 by Albert and David Viaplana ushered in a new era. It is now defined as a 'creativity centre' and focuses on Catalan art.
La Rambla 7, T 93 567 1110,
www.artssantamonica.cat

MACBA

Since its inauguration in 1995, the Museu d'Art Contemporani de Barcelona (MACBA) has anchored Raval's transformation from ghetto to multicultural epicentre. Richard Meier's typically white structure, clad in enamelled-steel panels, is defined on the plaza side (above) by a louvered glass facade, behind which a ramp connects the nine levels, and sculptural elements, such as the cut-out plane above the entrance that protrudes like an open drawer and an organic annexe. The permanent collection begins in the 1950s and features work by Catalans – Antoni Tàpies' 1993 *Rinzen* is a highlight – and global heavyweights. The upper floors house temporary exhibitions, such as local sculptor Sergi Aguilar's 2015 retrospective 'Reverse/Obverse' (overleaf).
Plaça dels Àngels 1, T 93 412 0810, www.macba.cat

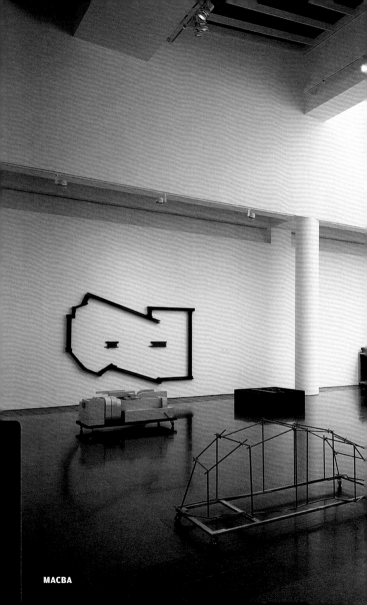

Galería Joan Prats

A pioneer of the art scene since 1976, the gallery represented Miró, Picasso, Moore and Christo in its former location on La Rambla de Catalunya. The establishment was one of hundreds affected by a 10-fold spike in overheads after a Franco-era rent control law ceased in early 2015, forcing businesses to close, downsize or move on. Joan Prats, which is named after its first exhibit four decades ago, relocated to its secondary space on nearby Carrer de Balmes, where it has complemented its roster of more prominent international names, including Norwegian Knut Åsdam, and Spanish notables, such as Victoria Civera and Alejandro Vidal, with younger talents – Hamburg artist Annika Kahrs showed 'Solid Surface' (above) in 2015. *Carrer de Balmes 54, T 93 216 0290, www.galeriajoanprats.com*

La Fábrica

Ricardo Bofill's La Fábrica, a converted factory that is now his studio and private residence, is nothing short of sublime in its melding of architectural and aesthetic modes. It is part brutalist vision, part romantic triumph, in its use of original concrete elements, retained for visual composition alone. It might also be part garden, as the tropical flora encroaches on the interiors, which he took to with a minimalist hand, mixing simple materials with high-tech furniture in the lofty, serene spaces. Within the eight silos are offices, archives, a large library and La Catedral (above), which is now an exhibition space displaying his architectural drawings and photographs of his numerous projects. Visit by appointment. The Bofill-designed Walden 7 is next door (see p076).
Avinguda de la Indústria 14

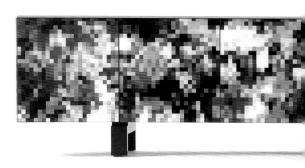

Cristian Zuzunaga

A cupboard for the digital age, Cristian Zuzunaga's riotous and visually chaotic 'Dreams' cabinet (above), €7,415, made for BD Barcelona Design (see p056), references his graphic design heritage in the form of the pixel. Established in 2007, Zuzunaga's studio, which creates bold, beautifully finished furniture and homewares, places import on artisanal processes and sustainable materials; a collection of merino wool cushions are handwoven by Teixidors (T 93 783 1199), a Terrassa-based firm. The watermelon-hued 'You and Me' tabletennis table, with iroko wood legs, is designed with RS Barcelona and doubles as a dining table; it's indicative of the fun and elegance inherent in his work. Select pieces are available at Roomservice (T 93 302 1016). *www.cristianzuzunaga.com*

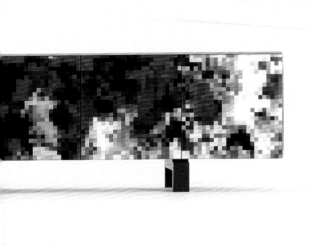

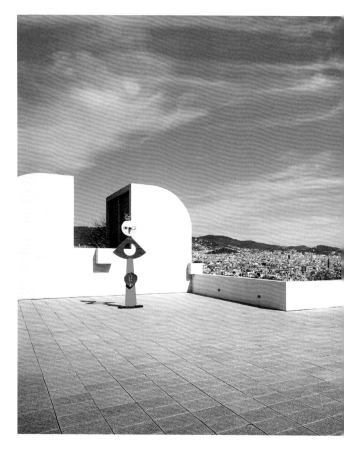

Fundació Joan Miró

Surrealist Joan Miró had his work mocked for many years in his home town, and it was only when he relocated to Paris that he achieved the recognition he deserved. Finally, in 1975 (when Miró was 82), he was honoured with this museum, housed in a rationalist building by architect Josep Lluís Sert. Its low-slung appearance belies the airy spaces within – ideal for Miró's vast canvases and sculptures (*The Caress of a Bird*, above left) – and its white walls and roof terraces dazzle in the sun. The Miró foundation hosts shows of modern artists too: Jackson Pollock, Mona Hatoum and Pipilotti Rist have featured in recent years, and Alexander Calder's *Mercury Fountain* has found a permanent home here. Closed Mondays, and Sundays from 2.30pm. *Parc de Montjuïc, T 93 443 9470, www.fmirobcn.org*

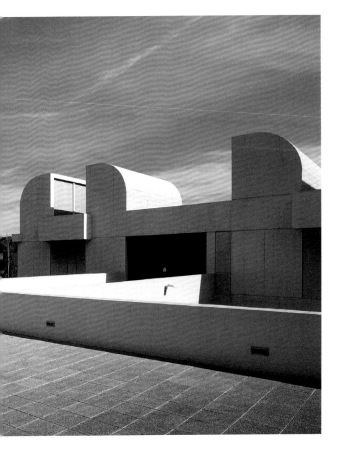

Fundació Antoni Tàpies

The Antoni Tàpies' foundation displays a huge variety of his work in many mediums, demonstrating the evolution of his oeuvre and the techniques and materials he used from the 1940s until his death in 2012. It is a fascinating collection that illustrates the influence of art movements, as well as world and personal events. It opened in 1990 in Lluís Domènech i Montaner's 1885 iron and brick building, topped by Tàpies' ethereal *Núvol i Cadira* (Cloud and Chair). A 2010 renovation emphasised its industrial nature (steel pillars and ornate balconies) and added exhibition space. A new pavilion is presided over by *Mitjó* (Sock) – a 3m replica of one of his unrealised sculptures (MNAC deemed it too simple to be art). Don't miss his mid-1950s matter paintings. *Carrer d'Aragó 255, T 93 487 0315, www.fundaciotapies.org*

La Place

French collector Anne-France Dujardin's studio/gallery morphs into the atelier of a visiting contemporary artist three times a year, followed by a two-week exhibition of their work. Past residents include 8GG, Sixtine Jacquart, Yasuko Fujioka and Alice Etcaetera, and you can observe them immersed in the creative process, almost as if it were a live installation. During the rest of the year, La Place sells artisanal, handmade pieces. The old lottery office was transformed in 2013, given a bright storefront with a timber entrance and polished concrete floors. An original brick wall divides public space from a kitchen and living quarters. Artworks hang from an iron frame, as do a series of vintage filing cabinets used to display jewellery. *Carrer de les Basses de Sant Pere 10, T 93 507 3700, www.laplace.es*

Museu Can Framis

The redevelopment of the working-class *barri* of Poblenou was most noteworthy for skyscrapers such as Torre Agbar (see p012), many built on land claimed at the expense of its industrial heritage. Museu Can Framis, a gallery for contemporary Catalan art, was a positive step in 2009. The conversion of an 18th-century wool factory is the work of BAAS, who installed a reinforced concrete annexe (above) alongside a pair of existing warehouses, creating a central courtyard. The gallery exhibits local art institution Fundació Vila Casas' permanent collection of more than 300 paintings, such as the work of Lita Cabellut (opposite, right) and Antoni Taulé (opposite, left); the museum's Espai Aø is dedicated to temporary shows. *Carrer de Roc Boronat 116-126, T 93 320 8736, www.fundaciovilacasas.com*

ARCHITOUR

A GUIDE TO BARCELONA'S ICONIC BUILDINGS

Barcelona has been engaged in a long love affair with architecture. However, in the past the city's affections were focused on just one man: Antoni Gaudí. These days it is far more profligate. A single regeneration project at Diagonal Mar attracted Jean Nouvel, EMBT, Dominique Perrault, MVRDV, Josep Lluís Mateo and Herzog & de Meuron. Yet since the financial crisis, such mega-developments have come to symbolise the excesses of a bygone era – the Ciutat de La Justícia (see p074) and Richard Rogers' mall fashioned from the Las Arenas bullring (Gran Vía de les Corts Catalanes 373-385, T 93 289 0244) were among the few that survived.

Since then, much has changed, if at a slower pace, and smaller in scale. The endless gentrification of the old city began on a high with the Mercat de Santa Caterina (Avinguda de Francesc Cambó 16, T 93 319 5740) and inspired similar projects, such as the Mercat dels Encants (opposite) and the restitution of the Mercat del Ninot (Carrer de Mallorca 133-157) pavilion by Mateo. It has continued to dazzle with more civic builds becoming neighbourhood icons, including Sant Gervasi's Biblioteca Joan Maragall (Carrer de Sant Gervasi de Cassoles 85), by local architects BCQ; Sant Antoni's Biblioteca Joan Oliver (Carrer del Comte Borrell 44-46), by RCR; BOPBAA's overhaul of El Molino theatre (Carrer de Vilà i Vilà 99, T 93 205 5111) in Poble Sec; and the Filmoteca (see p078) in Raval. *For full addresses, see Resources.*

Mercat dels Encants

The shiny refit of Barcelona's fleamarket belies its medieval origins. Occupying various locations over the centuries, it was relocated here in 1928, and revamped in 2013 as the harbinger of Les Glòries, which has been reborn as a landscaped public space now that traffic has been rerouted underground. The mirrored canopy by architects b720 provides shelter, but many locals lament that it has introduced an ill-conceived flashiness and ordered layout to what was once endearingly chaotic. The soaring kaleidoscopic roof of gilded steel panels reflects scenes of the stalls, which wrap around an auction area where gypsy traders still hustle. Visit either early in the morning or later in the day to appreciate the frenetic singsong of the hawkers, from which the market takes its name.
T 93 246 3030, www.encantsbcn.com

Ciutat de la Justícia

Barcelonians who appreciate very good architecture — in addition to all those unfortunates who face the prospect of navigating Spain's highly complicated legal system — are delighted that David Chipperfield's vast Ciutat de la Justícia (City of Justice) didn't get canned, as so many other large-scale projects did, when the fallout of the global economic meltdown hit the country. Positioned at Barcelona's westernmost point of entry, the complex comprises nine buildings, and accommodates law courts and public offices relating to the bar and forensic practices, arranging together what was previously a set of 17 different edifices widely dispersed across the city. Spacious plazas and a connecting concourse add to the ease of cross-communication here.
Gran Via de les Corts Catalanes

Walden 7
Situated on the city's periphery, Walden 7 is an early work by architect Ricardo Bofill – who designed the W Hotel (see p013) and La Fábrica (see p063) – and for many it is also his best. Completed in 1974, the russet-coloured building looms like a modernist fortress. Inside, the modular apartments are linked by a web of elevated walkways and bridges.
Carretera Reial 106, www.walden7.com

Filmoteca de Catalunya

The unassuming raw concrete facade of architect Josep Lluís Mateo's film archive HQ, opened here in 2011, blends in with its rundown surroundings. However, the building does have plenty of interest; it is cantilevered at either end due to unevenly stacked floors, and there are cinematic metaphors in the wide perforated screens of white steel and rust-hued Cor-ten (a colour that evokes analog film) that filter glare and provide privacy. The basalt stonework of the square melds into the foyer and ticket hall, and escalators lead down to two screening rooms, and up to the library and exhibition areas, which are bathed in natural light. Yet it will take more than an iconic structure to revive this still rather down-at-heel patch of the city. *Plaça Salvador Seguí 1-9, T 93 567 1070, www.filmoteca.cat*

Edifici Gas Natural

As happened with the Mercat de Santa Caterina (see p072), architect Benedetta Tagliabue realised the completion of the Edifici Gas Natural, the head office of the energy supplier, after the untimely death of her husband and working partner, Enric Miralles. Standing tall at the crossroads of Barceloneta, the old maritime district, and the modern Vila Olímpica, this bold 2008 building is very much the sum of its parts: an 85m-high tower; a 40m-long annexe, nicknamed the 'aircraft carrier', which cantilevers off the side; and a five-storey axis in-between (we recommend viewing it from all sides in order to best appreciate the unusual geometry). Its curtain-wall facade mirrors the nearby skyscrapers, among which are the mixed-use Torre Mapfre and Hotel Arts (see p016).
Plaça del Gas 1

SHOPS

THE BEST RETAIL THERAPY AND WHAT TO BUY

An excursion to any cultural or culinary hotspot in Barcelona should always be combined with some targeted retail therapy, as specialist boutiques are spread all over town. Born is great for fashion; head to Ivori (Carrer dels Mirallers 7, T 65 750 0041) for womenswear and Jää swimwear, and to Le Swing (Carrer del Rec 16, T 93 310 1449) for the best of vintage. In Eixample, there is chic menswear at The Outpost (Carrer del Rosselló 281, T 93 457 7137), and close by Cristina Castañer (Carrer del Rosselló 230, T 93 414 2428) has specialised in the most Mediterranean of footwear, the espadrille, since 1927, and has a new Benedetta Tagliabue-designed flagship. Concept store Trait (Carrer del Parlament 28, T 93 667 1631) carries urbanwear for men and women, as well as accessories and books.

For design, head to AOO (see p084) or Mar de Cava (Carrer de València 293, T 93 458 5333), which purveys furniture and objects by Lobster's Day, Paola Navone and Xavier Mañosa (opposite). La Central del Raval (Carrer d'Elisabets 6, T 90 080 2109) is one of the city's best bookshops; for art and design tomes, visit MACBA Store Laie (see p059) or the great *llibreria* at the Col·legi d'Arquitectes (Plaça Nova 5, T 93 306 7803). For epicurean gifts, pick up Catalan delights in the basement of El Corte Inglés (Plaça de Catalunya 14, T 93 306 3800) and discover Spanish wines at the family-run Vila Viniteca (Carrer dels Agullers 7, T 90 232 7777).
For full addresses, see Resources.

Apparatu

A studio and workshop in Rubí, which is a half-hour drive north of the city, Apparatu is headed by Joan Mañosa, a master potter for 40 years, his wife Aurora and their son Xavier, who returned to the family business after five years away in Berlin. The modular 'Pussel' (above), €280, which functions as a candleholder, vase or lamp, depending on the way that you assemble the ceramic pieces, was conceived as a game played by 12-year-old Xavier and his father. The work of Apparatu is often joyful; a range of classically shaped glazed white vases, 'Johnny 1', is clad in Joan's pop-culture sticker collection, and the 'Fang' table has wobbly-looking porcelain stoneware legs in pastel colours. Find pieces at AOO (see p084) or visit by appointment. *Passeig de la Riera 222, T 93 675 0105, www.apparatu.com*

Two Thirds

The name refers to the proportion of the planet covered by water, which is what this Basque-born brand strives to protect with its eco-friendly, grown-up surfwear, featuring sea-inspired motifs and patterns, and made using organic cotton and biodegradable materials. The retro-inspired boards are designed for Med conditions.
Carrer del Duc 8, T 93 250 9081

AOO

Marc Morro and Oriol Villar's shop/atelier is dedicated to the exaltation of simple, functional products and furniture, echoed by Arquitectura-G's clean interior design of sisal and slate. AOO is an acronym for 'Altrescosas Otrascosas Otherthings' and it purveys a carefully edited collection of homewares and objects by international artisans and Catalan designers – Miguel Milá, Rafael Marquina, André Ricard – as well as its own pieces, crafted largely from hardwood. Much of it will inspire a beach holiday, or at least a siesta. The 'Pepitu' deckchair is constructed from beechwood and has a boldly coloured linen back, and a series of rattan cane chairs are handmade in Valencia. We liked the Midori notebooks and Apparatu ceramics (see p081).
Carrer Sèneca 8, T 93 250 8254,
www.altrescoses.cat

Oriol Balaguer

Known as the Christian Lacroix of cake and chocolate-making, Oriol Balaguer has won many awards, yet he remains an aloof, serious figure within the tight-knit world of Spanish haute cuisine. Balaguer has a second store in Madrid, but his first was this bijou corner shop in well-heeled Barrio Alto. Inside, tarts, pastries, chocolates and mousses of the most intricate sculptural forms and flavours are presented with the sort of reverence usually reserved for precious jewels, thanks to high-impact displays, sleek packaging, spotlighting and even dry-ice effects. Purchase a tray of sweet treats and sweetmeats and a bottle of chilled cava, then retire to the nearby Parc Turó for an indulgent picnic.
*Plaça de Sant Gregori Taumaturg 2,
T 93 201 1846, www.oriolbalaguer.com*

Alfred Kerbs

Handmade in Italy, the eyewear of Alfred Kerbs melds on-trend styles with classic, laidback elegance. Traditional shapes are given an avant-garde twist, such as the 'Bat' sunglasses (above), €170, featuring blue-grey gradient Zeiss lenses and an irregular navy frame by master acetate manufacturer Mazzucchelli. 'Le Chat' is halfway between the cult cat-eye and futurism: the gradient black, taupe or tortoiseshell frame is entirely covered by a full-screen lens. Alfred Kerbs is stocked at high-end optician Les Lunettes, in Born (T 93 268 9870) and on Passeig de Gràcia (T 93 488 3688). More fashion specs can be found in the Kaleos (T 93 200 7478) flagship store on Muntaner – the boutique optometrist sells frames by the likes of Super, Miu Miu, Moscot and Celine. *www.alfredkerbs.com*

Loewe

Luxury Spanish leather brand Loewe has its Barcelona flagship in what was already a spectacular space within modernista architect Lluís Domènech i Montaner's Casa Lleó Morera. A fantastical stuccoed building, it was renovated in 2012. New York-based architect and designer Peter Marino is responsible for the interiors, which now feature a vertical garden and floors paved with slabs of Madagascan and Tanzanian stone; some of the original elements are still visible, especially in the frescoed ceilings. The brand's identity was also overhauled, in 2014, by then newly appointed creative director JW Anderson, who worked with graphic duo M/M Paris. Loewe's reinvented luggage, fashion and accessories are spread over three floors. *Passeig de Gràcia 35, T 93 216 0400, www.loewe.com*

BOO
This warm, offbeat concept store sells tailored garments with a nostalgic bent, as well as objects, books and perfume. Look for basics from Bleu de Paname and Saint James, and thoughtfully sourced local items, including Après Ski jewellery and Medwinds linen pieces. A penchant for deer figurines adds charming detail to the 1930s-inspired interiors.
Carrer de Bonavista 2, T 93 368 1458

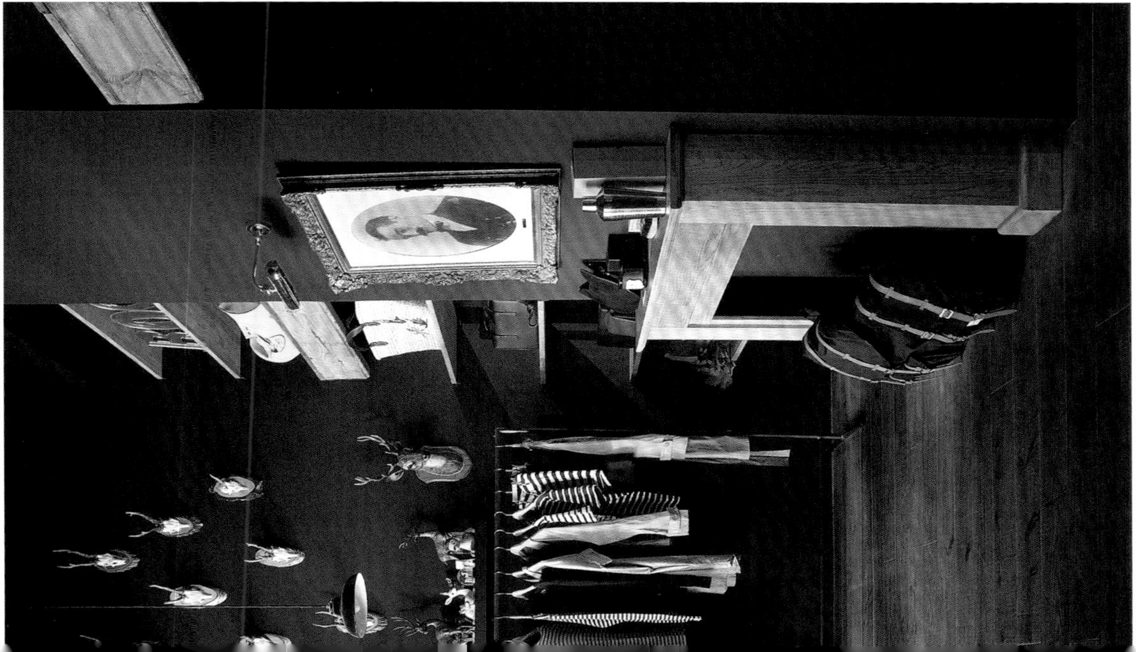

Idò DO Balear

This breezy, inviting bakery/deli/eaterie specialises in delights from the Balearics. On pine shelving you'll find items such as Mallorcan *sobrassada*, a cured and spiced sausage, Menorcan Mahón jams, cheeses, olives and organic wine, Gori de Muro artisan *marineras* biscuits and *ensaimada*, a sugar-dusted spiral pastry best enjoyed with your morning coffee. Take a seat on a wooden stool or log bench on the shaded front verandah, where whitewashed limestone walls and pebblestone paving conjure up an island vernacular, to sample the tidy lunch or dinner menu. Idò's specialities are *pamboli* – bread with garlic, olive oil and tomato – with ham and a chilled *pomada* (Xoriguer gin with lemonade). *Carrer de Viladomat 43, T 93 423 9627, www.idobalear.com*

Les Topettes

Owned by two young Spaniards who have combined their passion for design with a love of all things fragrant, Les Topettes is a bright perfumery stocking products from across the globe. Despite the small space, owners Lucía Laurin and Oriol Montañés have created a stylish modern interior, featuring glazed white bricks, vintage lamps and Macael marble floors. It's a joy to browse and ideal if you are in need of an elegant gift to take home. Choose an Etat Libre d'Orange fragrance, or a candle from Madrid-based perfume house Oliver & Co (above), €50 each. Men are well catered for with smart toiletries by Musgo Real, and for the eco-conscious, there are beautifully packaged organic candles from Spanish brand Olivia.

Carrer de Joaquín Costa 33,
T 93 500 5564, www.lestopettes.com

ESCAPES

WHERE TO GO IF YOU WANT TO LEAVE TOWN

Although Barcelona's beaches and Montjuïc park provide respite from the urban hustle, a day in the country or on the Costa Brava offers a superior breather. A trip to the Teatre-Museu Dalí (Plaça Gala-Salvador Dalí 5, T 97 267 7500) in Figueres can be combined with a visit to the artist's home in Cadaqués (Portlligat, T 97 225 1015; booking essential). Montserrat's craggy cliffs and monastery are a must for nature lovers and rock climbers; Catalonia's wine country, the Penedès, is just beyond. Take the train to the town of Vilafranca to tour the fin-de-siècle bodegas of cava producer Codorníu (Avinguda Jaume de Codorníu, Sant Sadurní d'Anoia, T 93 891 3342), and stay at Can Bonastre (Carretera B-224, km13.2, Masquefa, T 93 772 8767), a luxury resort ringed by vineyards.

For some sea air, travel south-west to gay-friendly Sitges, or north-east to Sant Pol de Mar, home of the celebrated Restaurant Sant Pau (Carrer Nou 10, T 93 760 0662; closed Sunday, Monday and Thursday lunchtimes). An hour north-east by train is Girona (see p100). The countryside that surrounds it is dotted with lovely villages and little-known gems, including hotel Mas de Torrent (Afores de Torrent, T 90 255 0321). In winter, the Vall de Núria offers gentle skiing, and further north, the Pyrenean town of Puigcerdà, and in particular Villa Paulita (Avinguda Pons i Gasch 15, T 97 288 4622), is a cosy base from which to head out on ski trips.
For full addresses, see Resources.

Caro Hotel, Valencia

Francesc Rifé Studio has given the former palace of the marquis of Caro a super-sleek interior while incorporating original sections of the city's Roman and Arab walls. The lobby is adorned with ceramics from the 10th- to 18th-century, though everything else is bang up to date, such as the marble bar and staircase, 26 rooms, the Rifé-designed furniture, fabricated by local firm Ziru, a skinny plunge pool, and the elegant Alma del Temple restaurant (above), which serves Mediterranean dishes. Valencia itself is a showcase of native architect Santiago Calatrava's work; the fantastical Ciudad de las Artes y las Ciencias (T 90 210 0031), with its orbed glass facade and white mosaics, is perhaps his most accomplished. *Almirall 14, T 96 305 9000, www.carohotel.com*

Consolación, Matarranya

A three-hour drive from Barcelona, in the pine-clad hills of the Matarranya on the borders of Catalonia and Aragón, is the Consolación hotel. A sensitively restored 16th-century hermitage forms the backbone of a building consisting of modern bedrooms, an accomplished restaurant and a library. Distributed around the grounds, however, are the main attraction: the Kubes (pictured).

These are guest rooms in the guise of gravity-defying, glass-fronted boxes tacked to the hillside, with views over the treetops. Interiors are minimal yet supremely comfortable, and each Kube has a sunken black slate bath to facilitate the ultimate recovery after exploring the surrounding landscape. *Carretera Nacional 232, km96, T 97 885 6755, www.consolacion.com.es*

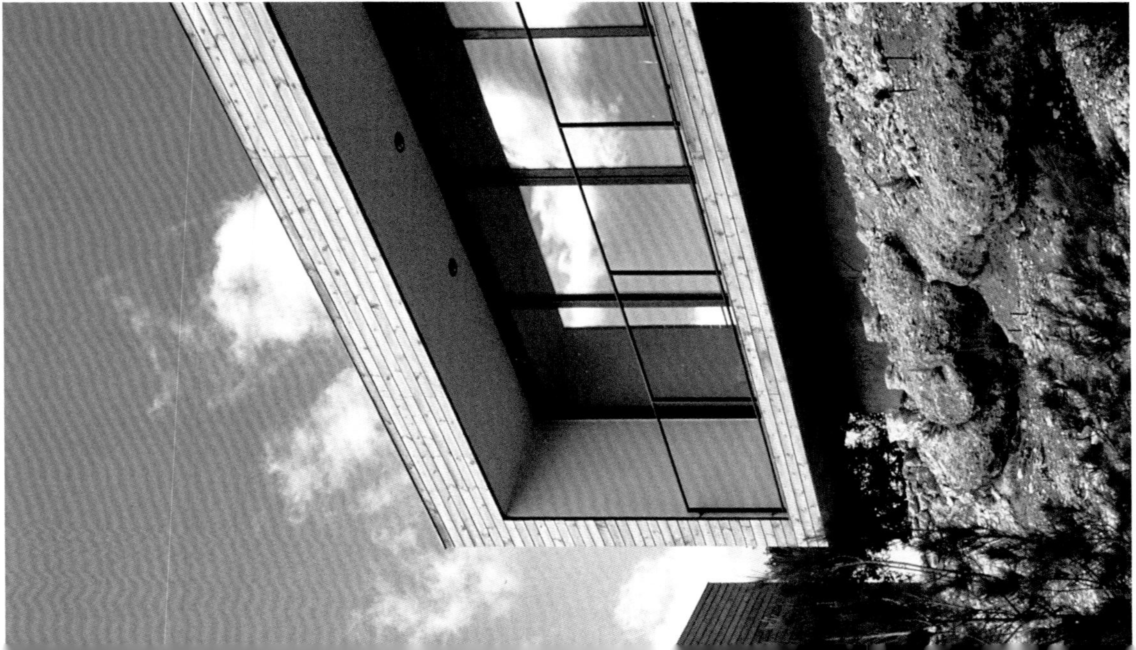

Alemanys 5, Girona

When Barcelona architect Anna Noguera and her husband set about transforming a 16th-century house into two apartments, they retained sections of original Roman stone and married the oatmeal-coloured walls to heavy steel doors and oak floors. Apartment El Baidu (above and opposite) has three bedrooms, a poured concrete bathroom with a bespoke tub designed by Noguera, and an expansive terrace that overlooks a lush courtyard and a sliver of the plunge pool. Views extend as far as Girona's medieval quarter, one of the best preserved Jewish ghettoes in Europe. Modish three-Michelin-starred restaurant El Celler de Can Roca (T 97 222 2157) is located just across the river in an annexe attached to a stone *masia* (farmhouse). *Carrer Alemanys 5, T 64 988 5136, www.alemanys5.com*

Santuari de Meritxell, Andorra
Sheltered in the forested mountains of Andorra, Ricardo Bofill's 1976 sanctuary is a three-hour drive north-west of the city. Its Romanesque-inspired sculpted colonnade, vaulted arches, tremendous slate steps, concaved amphitheatre and monastic, monochrome interiors make for a truly spiritual experience, whether you are visiting on pilgrimage or not.
Carretera de Meritxell, T 37 685 1253

NOTES

SKETCHES AND MEMOS

RESOURCES

CITY GUIDE DIRECTORY

A

AOO 084
Carrer Sèneca 8
T 93 250 8254
www.altrescoses.cat

Apparatu 081
Passeig de la Riera 222
Rubí
T 93 675 0105
www.apparatu.com

Las Arenas de Barcelona 072
Gran Vía de les Corts Catalanes 373-385
T 93 289 0244
www.arenasdebarcelona.com

Artevistas 056
Passatge del Crèdit 4
T 93 513 0465
www.artevistas-gallery.com

Arts Santa Mònica 058
La Rambla 7
T 93 567 1110
www.artssantamonica.cat

B

Bar Cañete 032
Carrer de la Unió 17
T 93 270 3458
www.barcanete.com

Bar Nou 036
Ronda Universitat 13
T 93 667 0506
www.barnou.cat

Barton 033
Carrer de Londres 103
T 93 414 5929
www.bartonbcn.com

Batuar 021
Cotton House Hotel
Gran Vía de les Corts Catalanes 670
T 93 450 5046
www.hotelcottonhouse.com

BD Barcelona Design 056
Carrer de Ramon Turró 126
T 93 457 0052
www.bdbarcelona.com

Bellavista 054
Mirador Forestal
Parc de l'Orenata
T 60 074 8470
www.grupbellavista.es

Biblioteca Joan Maragall 072
Carrer de Sant Gervasi de Cassoles 85
T 93 417 8347
www.bibliotecavirtual.diba.cat

Biblioteca Joan Oliver 072
Carrer del Comte Borrell 44-46
T 93 329 7216

Bobby Gin 032
Carrer de Francisco Giner 47
T 93 368 1892
www.bobbygin.com

Boca Grande 039
Passatge de la Concepció 12
T 93 467 5149
www.bocagrande.cat

Bodega 1900 024
Carrer de Tamarit 91

BOO 090
Carrer de Bonavista 2
T 93 368 1458
www.boobcn.com

El Born Centre Cultural 009
Plaça Comercial 12
T 93 256 6851
elborncentrecultural.barcelona.cat

The Box Social 018
Hotel Brummell
Nou de la Rambla 174
T 63 533 4453
www.theboxsocial.es

HOTELS

ADDRESSES AND ROOM RATES

Alemanys 5 100
Room rates:
Apartment El Baidu, from €250
Carrer Alemanys 5
Girona
T 64 988 5136
www.alemanys5.com

Hotel Arts 016
Room rates:
double, from €425
Carrer de la Marina 19-21
T 93 221 1000
www.hotelartsbarcelona.com

Axel Hotel 016
Room rates:
double, from €105
Carrer d'Aribau 33
T 93 323 9393
www.axelhotels.com

Bagués Hotel 022
Room rates:
double, from €650;
Jewel Suite, from €3,150
La Rambla 105
T 93 343 5000
www.derbyhotels.com

Hotel Brummell 018
Room rates:
double, from €120
Nou de la Rambla 174
T 93 125 8622
www.hotelbrummell.com

Can Bonastre 096
Room rates:
double, from €280
Carretera B-224, km13.2
Masquefa
T 93 772 8767
www.canbonastre.com

Caro Hotel 097
Room rates:
double, from €140
Almirall 14
Valencia
T 96 305 9000

Hotel Claris 016
Room rates:
double, €600
Carrer de Pau Claris 150
T 93 487 6262
www.derbyhotels.com

Cotton House Hotel 020
Room rates:
double, from €200;
Cotton Room, from €365
Gran Via de les Corts Catalanes 670
T 93 450 5045
www.hotelcottonhouse.com

Consolación 098
Room rates:
Kube, from €250
Carretera Nacional 232, km96
Matarraña
Teruel
T 97 885 6755
www.consolacion.com.es

Hotel DO: Plaça Reial 023
Room rates:
double, €350;
Junior Suite, from €525
Plaça Reial 1
T 93 481 3666
www.hoteldoreial.com

Mas de Torrent 096
Room rates:
Garden Suite, from €195
Afores de Torrent
Girona
T 90 255 0321
www.mastorrent.com

Mercer Hotel 019
Room rates:
double, from €390;
Junior Suite, €640
Carrer dels Lledó 7
T 93 310 2387
www.mercerbarcelona.com

Hotel Omm 016
Room rates:
double, from €690
Carrer del Rosselló 265
T 93 445 4000
www.hotelomm.com

El Palauet 017
Room rates:
double, from €500;
Principal Tibidabo Suite, from €700
Passeig de Gràcia 113
T 93 218 0050
www.elpalauet.com

Praktik Hotel Bakery 016
Room rates:
double, from €90
Carrer de Provença 279
T 93 488 0061
www.hotelpraktikbakery.com

The Serras 016
Room rates:
double, from €220
Passeig de Colom 9
T 93 169 1868
www.hoteltheserrasbarcelona.com

Villa Paulita 096
Room rates:
double, from €185
Avinguda Pons i Gasch 15
Puigcerdà
T 97 288 4622
www.villapaulitahotel.com

Vincci Bit 016
Room rates:
double, from €180
Carrer de Josep Plà 69
T 93 165 7420
www.vinccihoteles.com

Vincci Gala 016
Room rates:
double, from €240
Ronda de Sant Pere 32
T 93 508 3200
www.vinccihoteles.com

W Hotel 013
Room rates:
double, from €650
Plaça de la Rosa dels Vents 1
T 93 295 2800
www.w-barcelona.com

yök Casa + Cultura 016
Room rates:
double, from €240
Carrer de Trafalgar 39
T 64 062 5313
www.helloyok.com

WALLPAPER* CITY GUIDES

Executive Editor
Jeremy Case

Author
Ana Cañizares

Art Editor
Eriko Shimazaki

Photography Editor
Elisa Merlo
Assistant Photography Editor
Nabil Butt

Sub-Editor
Belle Place

Editorial Assistant
Emilee Jane Tombs

Contributors
Sally Davies
Suzanne Wales

Interns
Phoebe Hill
Tolu Ogundipe
Joella Qingyi Kiu

Production Controller
Sophie Kullmann

Wallpaper*® is a
registered trademark
of Time Inc (UK)

First published 2006
Revised and updated
2008, 2009, 2010,
2011 and 2013
Eighth edition 2015

© Phaidon Press Limited

All prices and venue
information are correct at
time of going to press,
but are subject to change.

Original Design
Loran Stosskopf
Map Illustrator
Russell Bell

Contacts
wcg@phaidon.com
@wallpaperguides

More City Guides
www.phaidon.com/travel

Phaidon Press Limited
Regent's Wharf
All Saints Street
London N1 9PA

Phaidon Press Inc
65 Bleecker Street
New York, NY 10012

Phaidon® is a registered
trademark of Phaidon
Press Limited

www.phaidon.com

A CIP Catalogue record for
this book is available from
the British Library.

Printed in China

ISBN 978 0 7148 6930 8

PHOTOGRAPHERS

Eugeni Aguiló
Cristian Zuzunaga
cabinet, pp064-065

Fernando Alda
Caro Hotel, p097

Palmer Aldritch
43 The Spa, p030

Roger Casas
Barcelona city view,
inside front cover
Tres Chimeneas, p010
Torre de Comunicaciones
de Montjuïc, p011
Torre Agbar, p012
W Hotel, p013
Casa Milà, pp014-015
El Palauet, p017
Hotel Brummell, p018
Mercer Hotel, p019
Cotton House Hotel,
p020, p021
Bagués Hotel, p022
Hotel DO: Plaça Reial,
p023
Satan's Coffee Corner,
p025
CCCB, p026

Casa Batlló, p027
Pavelló Mies van der
Rohe, pp028-029
El Velódromo, p031
Barton, p033
Mitja Vida, p034, p035
Bar Nou, pp036-037
Dos Palillos, p038
Boca Grande, p039
Saboc, p040
Poncelet Cheese Bar, p041
Pakta, pp042-043
Disfrutar, p044, p045
Lando, pp046-047
Chivuo's, p048
Pez Vela, p049
Jaime Beriestain
Café, p050
Tickets, p051
Koy Shunka, pp052-053
Mireia Ruiz, p055
Disseny Hub, p057
Arts Santa Monica, p058
MACBA, p059, pp060-061
Galería Joan Prats, p062
La Fábrica, p063
Fundació Joan
Miró, pp066-067
Fundació Antoni
Tàpies, p068
La Place, p069
Museu Can Framis,
p070, p071

Mercat dels Encants, p073
Ciutat de la Justicia,
pp074-075
Filmoteca de
Catalunya, p078
Edifici Gas Natural, p079
Two Thirds, pp082-083
AOO, p084, p085
Oriol Balaguer, p086, p087
Loewe, p089
Boo, pp090-091
Idò DO Balear, p092, p093
Les Topettes, p094

Peartree Digital
Apparatu lamp, p081
Alfred Kerbs
sunglasses, p088
Oliver & Co candles, p095

Enric Duch
Alemanys 5, p100, p101

Pedro Pegenaute
Walden 7, pp076-077

BARCELONA

A COLOUR-CODED GUIDE TO THE HOT 'HOODS

EIXAMPLE
The heartland of modernista architecture should be the first port of call for Gaudí fans

BARRI GÒTIC
Barna's historic core is a warren of medieval lanes encircling the flamboyant cathedral

BARCELONETA
This salty, low-rise, maritime district is bordered by a collection of brave new skyscrapers

GRÀCIA
Often ignored by those en route to Gaudí's Parc Güell, yet Gràcia is full of lovely squares

POBLE SEC
It's still leafy and relatively chilled out, but this is perhaps the city's newest 'in' district

POBLENOU
Home to a nascent high-rise business district, and a new generation of loft-living locals

RAVAL
Now arguably Barcelona's cultural epicentre, Raval brims with cool bars and boutiques

SANT PERE/BORN
For top shopping and a sedate vision of the city as it used to be, head here. But do so fast

For a full description of each neighbourhood, see the Introduction.
Featured venues are colour-coded, according to the district in which they are located.